Lyndsey Christine

Kathryn Louise

Marcia Lynette

Bisque doll circa 1890

# Nana's Trunk

An old grey-shingled house sits high on the north bank of a Michigan lake. Each year it becomes a holiday home to six young cousins as they and their families travel to visit at the cottage built by their great great-grandparents. On the long sunny days of summer, the children swim, sail, ski or paddle the old canoe, rejoicing in being together, sharing secrets and found-objects. But should the day turn cool and rainy, they go off to the attic to pore through Nana's trunk. Here they can spend the day playing dress-up in the stored vintage clothing of long-ago relatives who were once the same ages as these cousins: Lyndsey, 2; Marcie, 4; Sean, 6; Patrick, 7; Aaron, 10; and Katie, 13.

The pine and leather steamer trunk holds children's clothing dating as far back as 1860. Most of these were home-sewn; there were few ready-to-wear store garments available to middle-class families. Young ladies' dresses mirrored those of their mothers. The fabrics were heavy and petticoats plentiful. In the 19th century, waists were expected to be tiny and corsetry was worn even by the very young. The cousins of today could neither be active nor comfortable while wearing the confining clothing of a century ago.

The transition of boy's fashions in Nana's trunk reflect the trends and fads of the times. In earlier days, little boys were first dressed in frocks, advancing to knicker suits until those long-awaited "first long pants." At the end of the 19th century, a revolution in children's clothing took place. "Physicians, social reformers, educators and mothers began to grasp that children's minds and bodies had needs different from adults. Among other things, clothing was now constructed that presented middle-class children not as parlor statues but as active, growing beings." said Nancy Villa Bryk, a curator of the Henry Ford Museum.

With the costumes carefully folded away and the lid lowered on the trunk, the children return to today's fashions. How many parents (and grandparents) have wished for a bit of that formality of dress from the past (and its incumbent good manners) as we witness the jeans and sweats worn for both recreational and social activities?

# Kathryn Louise

**1880**

**1880**

1. Katie models two blue gowns from 1880. The first is dressmaker-made, a shimmering silk-faille dress in royal blue, accented with pale blue velvet ribbons and ribbon rosettes.

2. The second is a peacock silk frock with oversized petal shaped sleeves and a mid-calf length skirt. The bodice features a square ruffled neckline and has a pinafore look. Both frocks are elegant, definitely designed for important occasions.

3. Katie loves the delicate charm of a 1912 white voile frock trimmed with tiny tucks, heavy embroidery and fabric buttons down the back. Girls' fashions of this era imitated the "S" look of their fashionable mothers and aunties. In 1912, Katie at 13 would have been wearing her long hair down. She wouldn't be allowed to put it "up" until her late teens when the hairbow would be traded for elaborate feathers, fruit, flowers or plumes.

**1912**

# Marcia Lynette

**1880**

**1900**

**1930**

4. Marcie's day-dress is of cretonne-lined plaid cotton and made with flared princesse lines. The front pleats and back bustle copy more mature styling. She carries a bisque doll which no longer has a stitch to wear!

5. Moving to the fashions of 1900, Marcie models a sheer white cotton frock, fully embroidered and designed with bolero effect. The cap sleeve, wrist, neck, belt and bolero are all edged with heavy cotton lace. In her hair she wears the oversized bow, so fashionable with girls from toddler through adolescent.

6. Lastly, Marcie delights in the brilliant colors of coral, yellow, blue and green embroidery on the sheer gauze dress from Hungary, made in 1930. The imported white dress might not follow the American style of the '30s but in it, she can pretend to tap dance and sing just like Shirley Temple.

# Lyndsey Christine

**1906**

**1893**

**1927**

7. Lyndsey dresses up in the 1893 Kate Greenaway style. Her fine blue cotton dress is trimmed with white bias bands, and in it, she poses prettily with a parasol.

8. In 1906, a doting aunt on a European tour sent her niece this unusual faille-like blue yoked dress, appliqued with seven different motifs. They include an Alpine hiker, elfin old man, and a barefoot boy! Lyndsey wears it while trying to balance the old hoop with her stick.

9. Lyndsey revels in the look and feel of the "Roaring Twenties" romper suit, which carries tiny rows of smocking and embroidery hand-done in blue and black on the cinnamon colored cotton. The female "look" of the Twenties was *Undeveloped Youth*: lots of leg was smart for mother and child. Might this play-tog have been Nana's?

Not to be outdone by the girls, the three boys find their rainy day fun in discovering what will fit them this year. Have they grown tall enough, shoulders filled out sufficiently to wear a favorite costume?

# Sean Hamilton

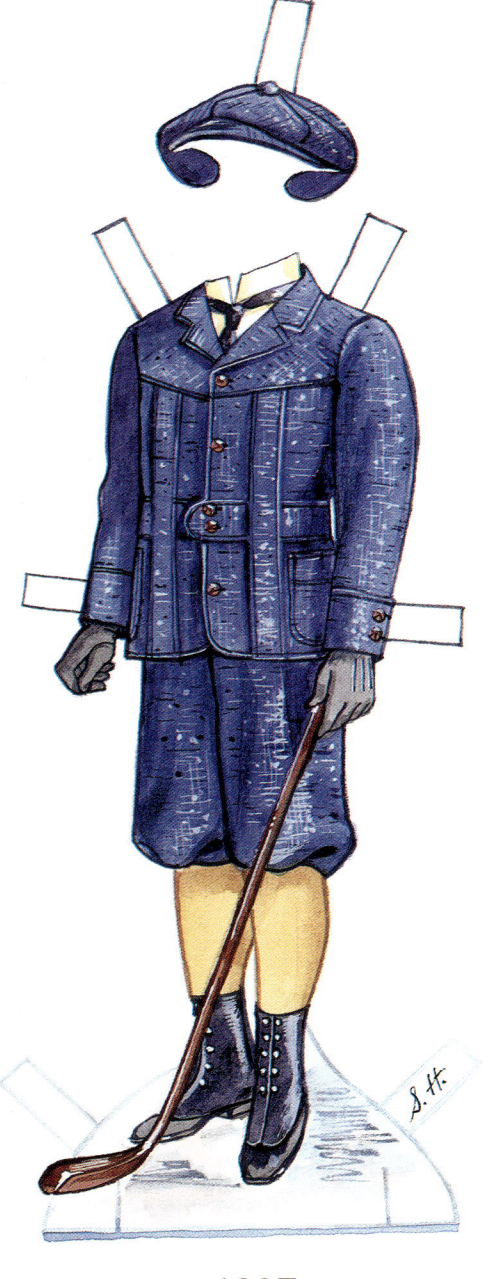

**1897**

**1910**

**1924**

10. Sean likes the way he looks in the 1897 blue tweed Norfolk suit, also known as the Tyrolean Hunter's suit. Box pleats frame the closure; the self-belt is buttoned, his cap matches. Made from a pattern in *The Delineator* magazine, this heavy suit will do for a winter's day of hockey.

11. Two of the boys' favorite choices are the exquisitely handsome ringbearer suits once worn in a family wedding at the turn of the 19th century. Sean gently slips on the delicate ecru pure silk shirt which is fashioned with vertical tucks and rows of moss green French knots. Tiny buttons fasten beneath a front closure panel. The shirt then buttons onto moss green shorts.

12. Sean, dressed for a birthday party, looks mighty fine in the 1924 black velvet Eton jacket and button-on shorts. The only embellishments are the pants pockets, perfect for hiding a frog to scare any girls at the party.

# Patrick Allan

**1910**

**1900**

**1900**

13. Cousin Patrick wears the twin suit, identical in every way but color, a soft shade of rose. The boys link arms and laugh as they stumble through "Here Comes the Bride."

14. Middy suits were popular with the boys of 1900! Here is another version, this time in a woolen tattersall plaid. Patrick thinks the elastic hems of the knickers are scratchy, but he likes the jaunty sailor cap and the Navy insignia on the sleeves.

15. Another sailor-type suit catches Patrick's eye. The group regards its 6 1/2 inch mother-of-pearl buttons as "awesome." The longish jacket and over-the-knee pants are of maroon wool; the sailor collar is uniquely styled with four points. Three self-buttons trim the lower pant leg.

# Aaron James

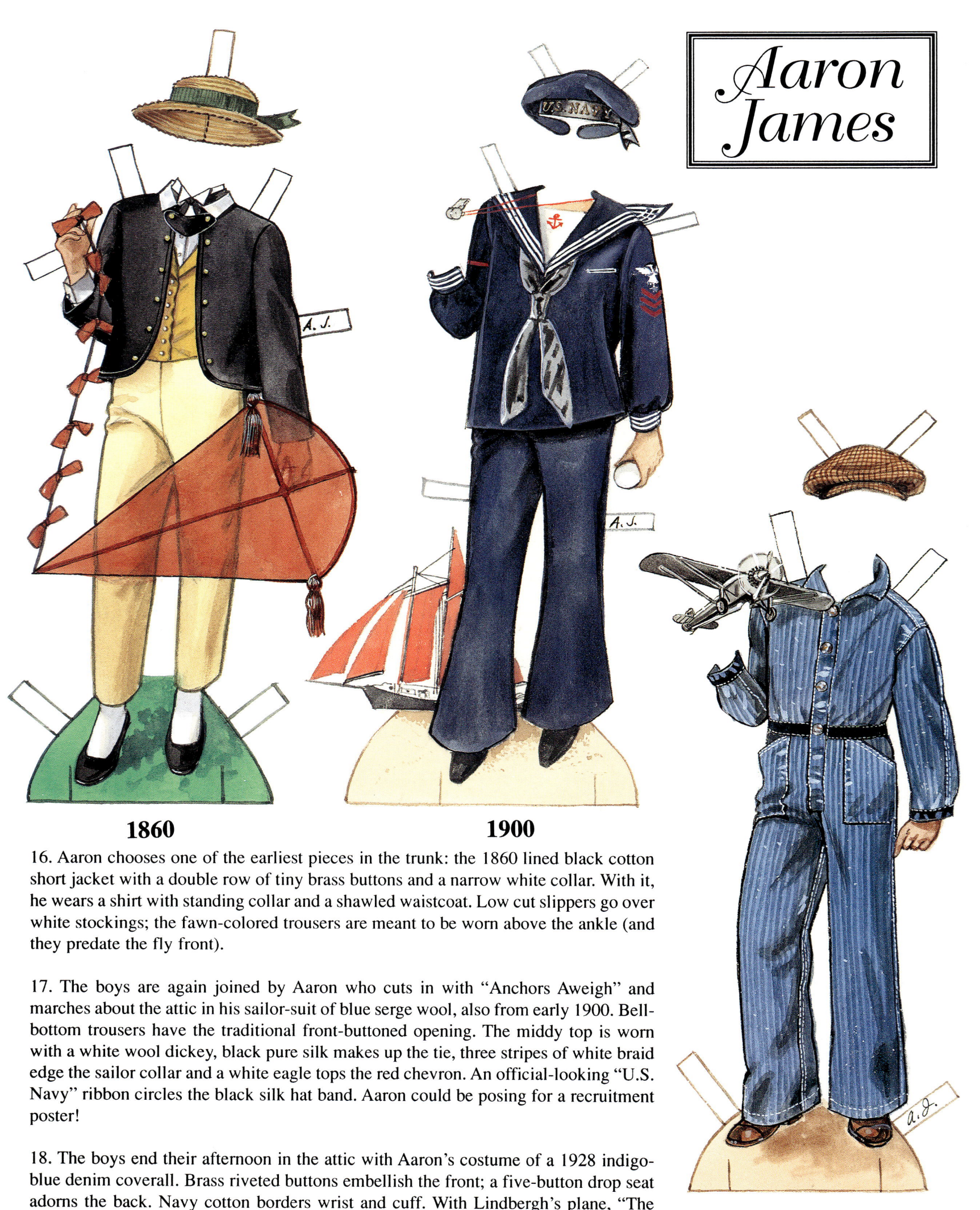

**1860**

**1900**

**1928**

16. Aaron chooses one of the earliest pieces in the trunk: the 1860 lined black cotton short jacket with a double row of tiny brass buttons and a narrow white collar. With it, he wears a shirt with standing collar and a shawled waistcoat. Low cut slippers go over white stockings; the fawn-colored trousers are meant to be worn above the ankle (and they predate the fly front).

17. The boys are again joined by Aaron who cuts in with "Anchors Aweigh" and marches about the attic in his sailor-suit of blue serge wool, also from early 1900. Bell-bottom trousers have the traditional front-buttoned opening. The middy top is worn with a white wool dickey, black pure silk makes up the tie, three stripes of white braid edge the sailor collar and a white eagle tops the red chevron. An official-looking "U.S. Navy" ribbon circles the black silk hat band. Aaron could be posing for a recruitment poster!

18. The boys end their afternoon in the attic with Aaron's costume of a 1928 indigo-blue denim coverall. Brass riveted buttons embellish the front; a five-button drop seat adorns the back. Navy cotton borders wrist and cuff. With Lindbergh's plane, "The Spirit of St. Louis," Aaron looks at home in the 1920s.

Child's chair circa 1920

Sled circa 1890

Metal truck circa 1930

Rocking horse circa 1900

For greater stability consider mounting accessories on light-weight cardboard.

Zeppelin "Los Angeles" circa 1930

Studebaker Junior Wagon circa 1910

Sean Hamilton

Aaron James

Patrick Allan